U.S.A. TRAVEL GUIDES

TEXAS

BY ANN HEINRICHS • ILLUSTRATED BY MATT KANIA

JAN 2021

The Child's World®
childsworld.com

Published by The Child's World®
1980 Lookout Drive • Mankato, MN 56003-1705
800-599-READ • www.childsworld.com

Photo Credits
Photographs ©: Shutterstock Images, cover, 1, 20, 24, 31,
32, 37 (top), 37 (bottom); Arina P. Habich/Shutterstock
Images, 7; CrackerClips Stock Media/Shutterstock
Images, 8; Oksana Perkins/Shutterstock Images, 11;
Ralf Broskvar/Shutterstock Images, 12; Kushal Bose/
Shutterstock Images, 15; Richard A. McMillin/Shutterstock
Images, 16; Yulia Davidovich/Shutterstock Images, 19;
Warren Price Photography/Shutterstock Images, 23;
Lisa Pessin Photography/Shutterstock Images, 27; Zoran
Orcik/Shutterstock Images, 28; Bob Pardue/Southwest/
Alamy, 35

ISBN 9781503819832
LCCN 2016961195

Printing
Printed in the United States of America
PA02334

Ann Heinrichs is the author
of more than 100 books
for children and young
adults. She has also enjoyed
successful careers as a
children's book editor and
an advertising copywriter.
Ann grew up in Fort Smith,
Arkansas, and lives in
Chicago, Illinois.

About the Author
Ann Heinrichs

Matt Kania loves maps and, as a
kid, dreamed of making them. In
school he studied geography and
cartography, and today he makes
maps for a living. Matt's favorite
thing about drawing maps is
learning about the places they
represent. Many of the maps
he has created can be found in
books, magazines, videos, Web
sites, and public places.

About the
Map Illustrator
Matt Kania

On the cover: The Alamo Mission is near San Antonio.

OUR TEXAS TRIP

Texas 4

Padre Island off the Gulf Coast 7

Wildlife in Big Bend National Park 8

Lubbock's Prairie Dogs 11

Ysleta del Sur Pueblo 12

San Antonio's Mission San José 15

Remember the Alamo! 16

Charro Days in Brownsville 19

Cowboys at the Elkins Ranch 20

The Texas State Fair in Dallas 23

The Poteet Strawberry Festival 24

The State Capitol in Austin 27

Kilgore's East Texas Oil Museum 28

Space Center Houston 31

The Bureau of Engraving and Printing in Fort Worth . . . 32

Odessa's Meteor Crater 35

Our Trip 36
State Symbols 37
State Song 37
State Flag and Seal 37
Famous People 38
Words to Know 38
To Learn More 39
Index 40

Ready for a trip through the Lone Star State? That's Texas! It's a mighty big state. That means you're in for a mighty big adventure!

What will you do in Texas? You'll visit a community of prairie dogs. You'll gather seashells and climb sand dunes. You'll see vintage spacesuits. And you'll learn why Texans remember the Alamo. Not bad for one state!

Are you ready? Then buckle up, and let's hit the road!

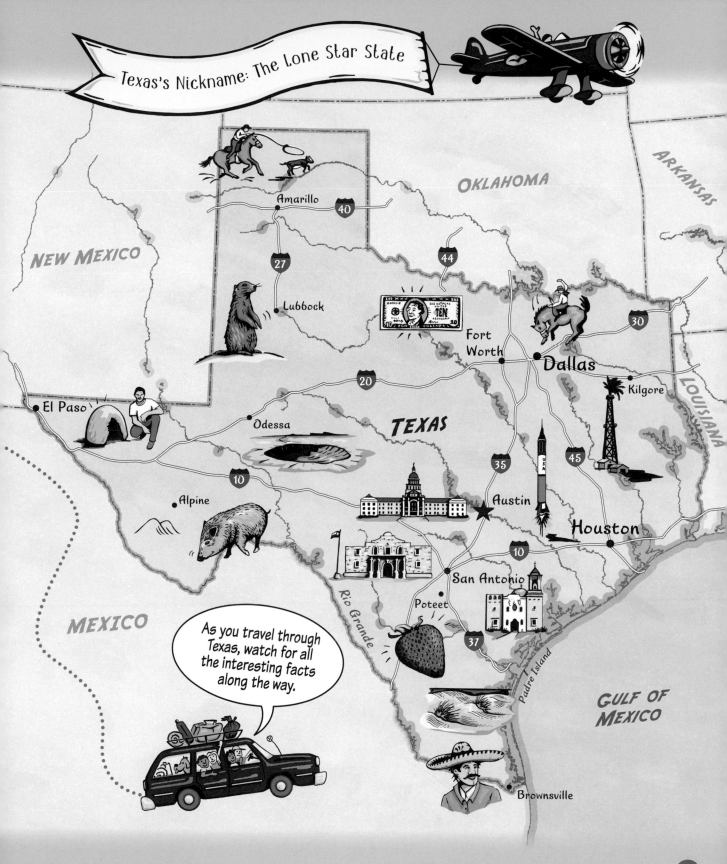

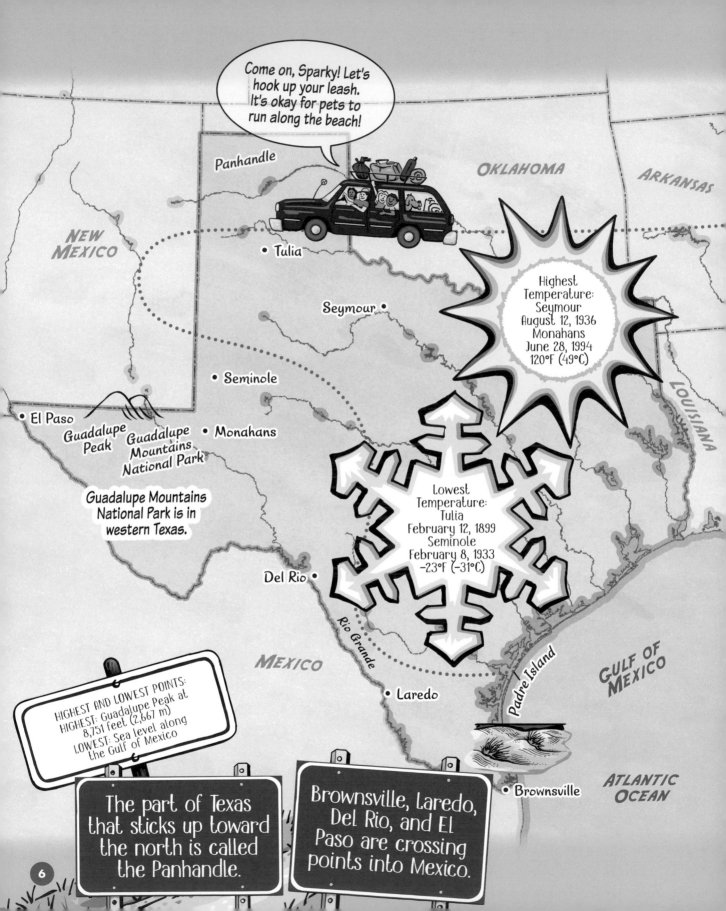

PADRE ISLAND OFF THE GULF COAST

Tumble down a sand dune. Gather seashells on the beach. You're exploring Padre Island National Seashore!

Padre Island is long and narrow. It's called a barrier island. That's a long island just off a coast. It protects the coast from big waves.

Texas is a huge state. Only Alaska has a bigger land area. Southeastern Texas faces the Gulf of Mexico. The gulf is part of the Atlantic Ocean. Pine forests cover eastern Texas. Grassy plains stretch across much of the state. In the west are mountains and deserts.

The Rio Grande is one of Texas's major rivers. It forms the southern border with Mexico.

Dip your toes in the water surrounding South Padre Island.

WILDLIFE IN BIG BEND NATIONAL PARK

Do you like seeing animals in the wild? Just roam around Big Bend National Park. It's along the Rio Grande south of Alpine. You'll see deer and coyotes. You might even spot mountain lions.

If you're camping out, prick up your ears. You may hear a snuffling sound at night. It could be a javelina looking for food. Javelinas are like wild pigs with bristly hair. Eek!

Lots of animals live off the coast. Sea turtles make their nests on the beaches. In the water, you'll see jellyfish and sharks.

The Rio Grande flows through Big Bend National Park.

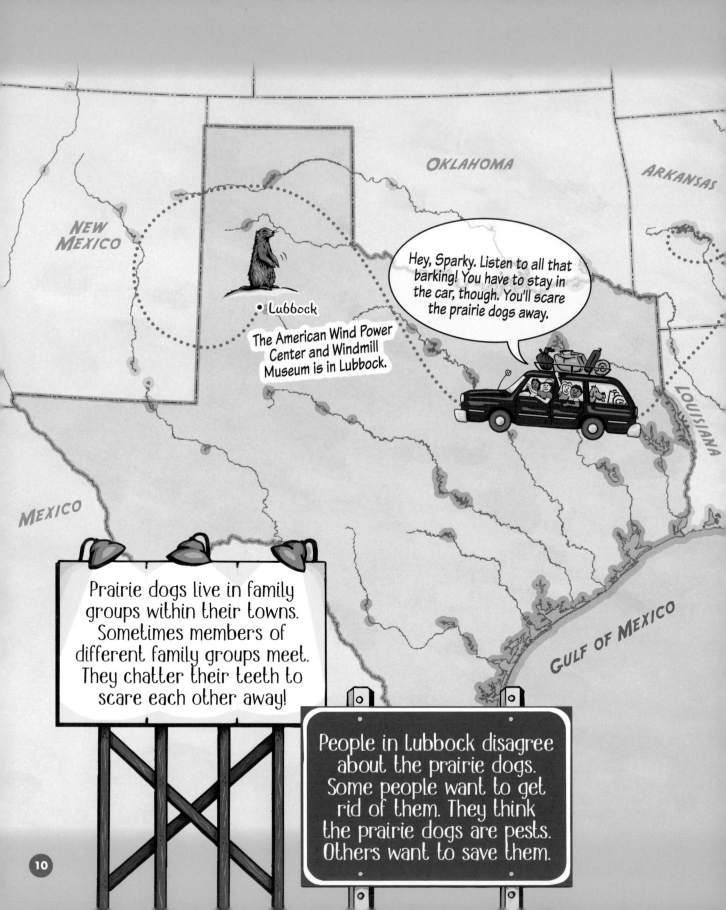

The American Wind Power Center and Windmill Museum is in Lubbock.

Hey, Sparky. Listen to all that barking! You have to stay in the car, though. You'll scare the prairie dogs away.

Prairie dogs live in family groups within their towns. Sometimes members of different family groups meet. They chatter their teeth to scare each other away!

People in Lubbock disagree about the prairie dogs. Some people want to get rid of them. They think the prairie dogs are pests. Others want to save them.

LUBBOCK'S PRAIRIE DOGS

Head out to the east of Lubbock. You'll find a huge prairie dog town. Thousands of the furry little critters live there!

Prairie dogs are social animals. They live in big communities. They dig long burrows, or tunnels, underground. That's where they live and raise their young.

Prairie dogs are related to squirrels and chipmunks. They often sit upright outside their holes. They make a barking sound when they're alarmed. That's how they got their name!

Burrowing owls live among the prairie dogs. The owls can't dig their own holes. They nest in the prairie dogs' burrows!

Prairie dogs spend much of their time building and rebuilding their underground homes.

YSLETA DEL SUR PUEBLO

Watch how the people bake bread. They use a *horno*, or beehive-shaped oven. Then enjoy a lively dance show. Finally, you can join in a friendship dance.

You're visiting Ysleta del Sur **Pueblo** at the Tigua Indian Cultural Center. It's located in a Tigua Native American community in El Paso.

More than ten Native American tribes once lived in Texas. Some were farmers. Those along the coast caught fish and shellfish. Others hunted buffalo across the plains. Today, the three tribes that live in Texas are the Alabama-Coushatta Tribe, the Kickapoo Traditional Tribe, and the Ysleta del Sur Pueblo.

Spanish explorers arrived in the 1500s. Later, Spanish priests began opening **missions**. They forced Native Americans to practice Christianity there. Ysleta began as a Spanish mission. It's the oldest settlement in Texas. The Tigua have lived there since 1682.

Hornos are made from sun-dried mud bricks.

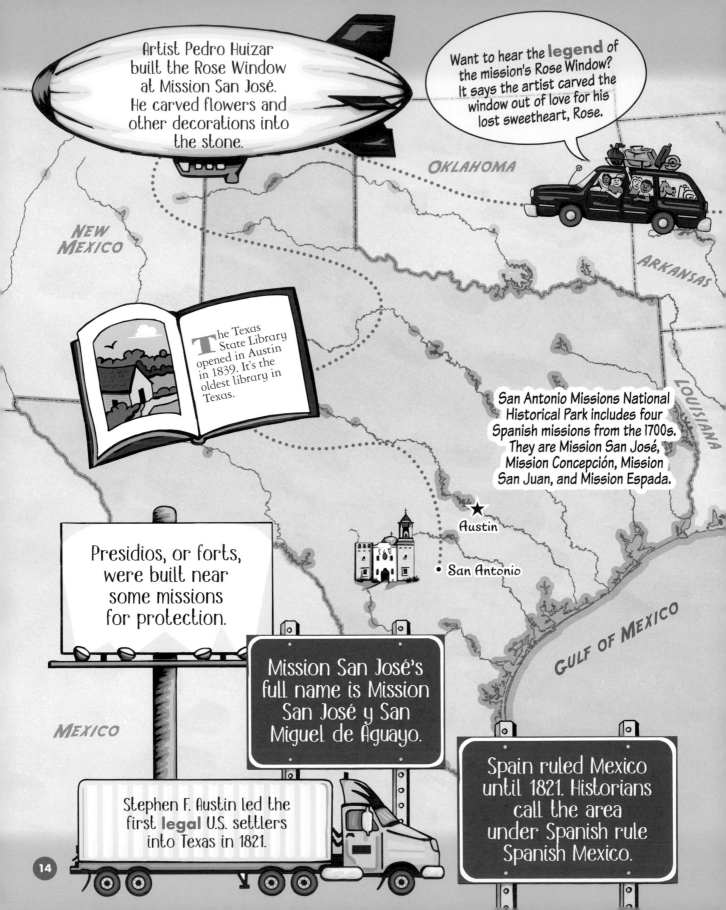

SAN ANTONIO'S MISSION SAN JOSÉ

Climb the winding steps of the church tower. Each step is carved from an oak log. See the building where grain was stored. It almost looks like a church, too.

You're visiting Mission San José in San Antonio. Missions were almost like small towns. They included vast fields and cattle herds. Native Americans did the farming and ranch work.

Mission San José opened in 1720. It was called the Queen of the Missions. About 300 Native Americans lived and worked there. Native Americans that lived in the mission were from different hunting and gathering groups. They were collectively known as the Coahuiltecans. They were forced to change their religion to Christianity and abandon their traditional way of life.

During this time, Texas was part of Spanish Mexico. Settlers began arriving from the United States. The first ones came in the early 1800s.

Mission San José was the largest mission in the San Antonio area.

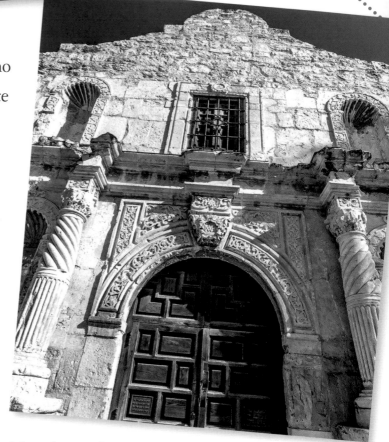

Be sure to visit the Alamo in San Antonio! A fierce battle took place there in 1836. Many Texans wanted freedom from Mexico. They fought the Texas Revolution. Freedom fighters were defending the Alamo. More than 180 people fought and died there. Then Texans wanted freedom even more. Their battle cry was "Remember the Alamo!"

Sam Houston led the final battle against Mexico. It was the Battle of San Jacinto. Then Texas became an independent country. It was called the Republic of Texas.

Texas soldiers defended the Alamo for 13 days before the Mexican army overpowered them.

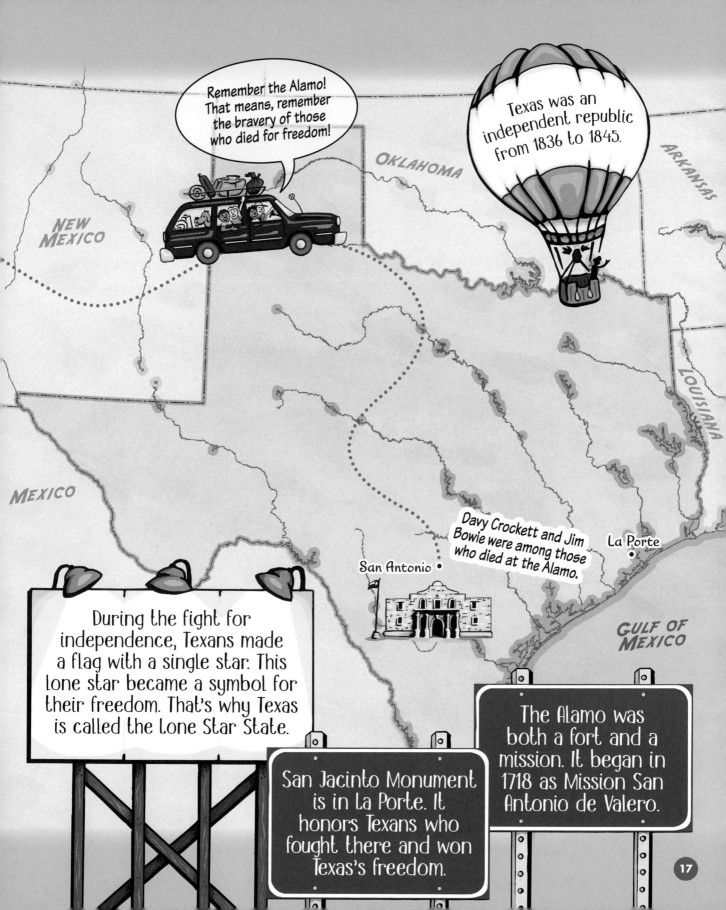

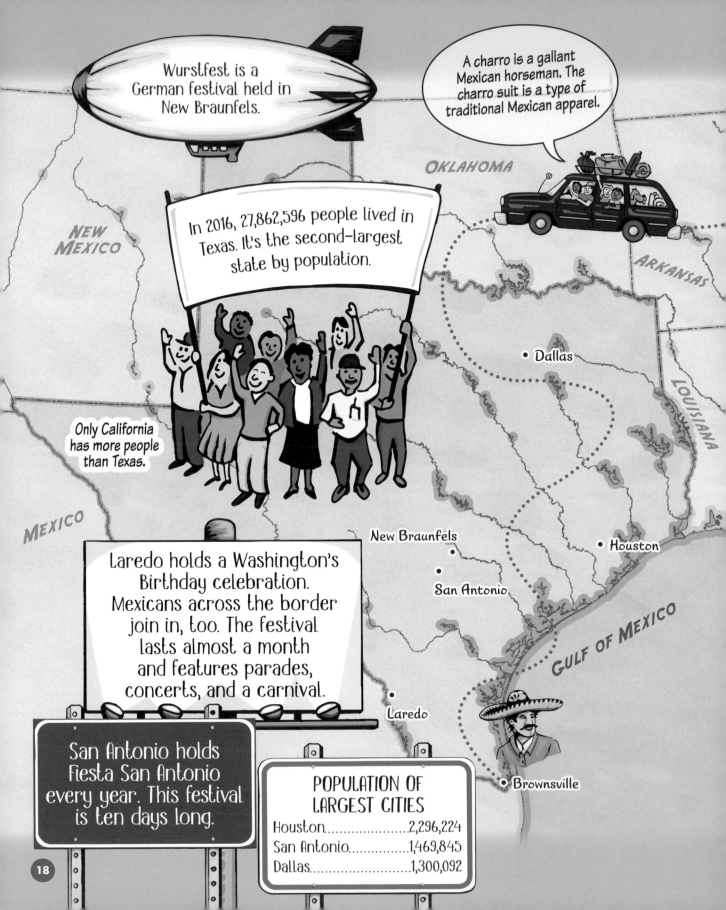

Wurstfest is a German festival held in New Braunfels.

A charro is a gallant Mexican horseman. The charro suit is a type of traditional Mexican apparel.

OKLAHOMA

ARKANSAS

NEW MEXICO

In 2016, 27,862,596 people lived in Texas. It's the second-largest state by population.

Only California has more people than Texas.

MEXICO

LOUISIANA

• Dallas

• Houston

New Braunfels

San Antonio

GULF OF MEXICO

Laredo holds a Washington's Birthday celebration. Mexicans across the border join in, too. The festival lasts almost a month and features parades, concerts, and a carnival.

Laredo

Brownsville

San Antonio holds Fiesta San Antonio every year. This festival is ten days long.

POPULATION OF LARGEST CITIES
Houston....................2,296,224
San Antonio...............1,469,845
Dallas........................1,300,092

CHARRO DAYS IN BROWNSVILLE

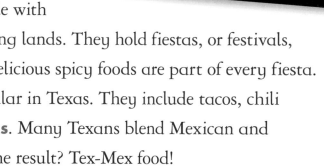

Girls and women wear ruffly dresses. Boys and men wear sombreros. Those are big Mexican hats. Everyone's clothing is brilliantly decorated. It's time for Charro Days in Brownsville!

Charro Days is a big Mexican American festival. People in Matamoras, Mexico, join in, too. That city is right across the border.

Hispanics are people with roots in Spanish-speaking lands. They hold fiestas, or festivals, throughout the year. Delicious spicy foods are part of every fiesta. Mexican foods are popular in Texas. They include tacos, chili peppers, and **enchiladas**. Many Texans blend Mexican and U.S. food **traditions**. The result? Tex-Mex food!

Tex-Mex is a popular style of American food.

COWBOYS AT THE ELKINS RANCH

Climb aboard a jeep with horns on the front. Then ride out across the range. The cowboys put on a show. You're at the Elkins Ranch near Amarillo!

Cowboys are a big part of Texas **culture**. Many new settlers in Texas started cattle ranches. They hired cowboys to do the ranch work.

The Texas Rangers were officially organized in 1835. These horseback lawmen kept peace and protected settlers. Texas Rangers still keep peace in Texas today!

At the Elkins Ranch, you'll get to experience what cowboy life is like.

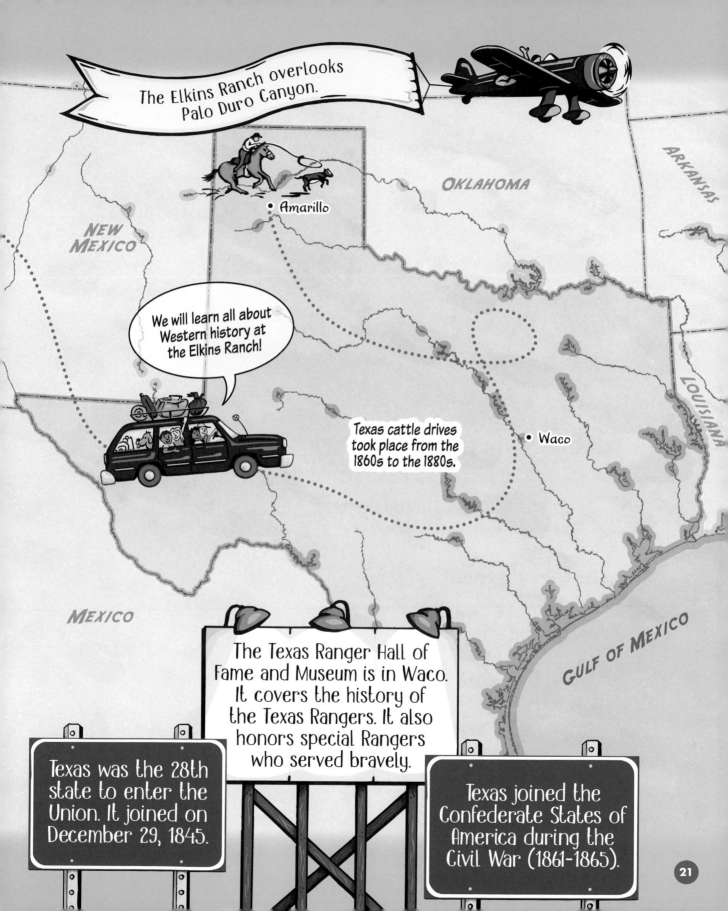

The Elkins Ranch overlooks Palo Duro Canyon.

OKLAHOMA

ARKANSAS

NEW MEXICO

• Amarillo

We will learn all about Western history at the Elkins Ranch!

Texas cattle drives took place from the 1860s to the 1880s.

• Waco

LOUISIANA

MEXICO

GULF OF MEXICO

The Texas Ranger Hall of Fame and Museum is in Waco. It covers the history of the Texas Rangers. It also honors special Rangers who served bravely.

Texas was the 28th state to enter the Union. It joined on December 29, 1845.

Texas joined the Confederate States of America during the Civil War (1861-1865).

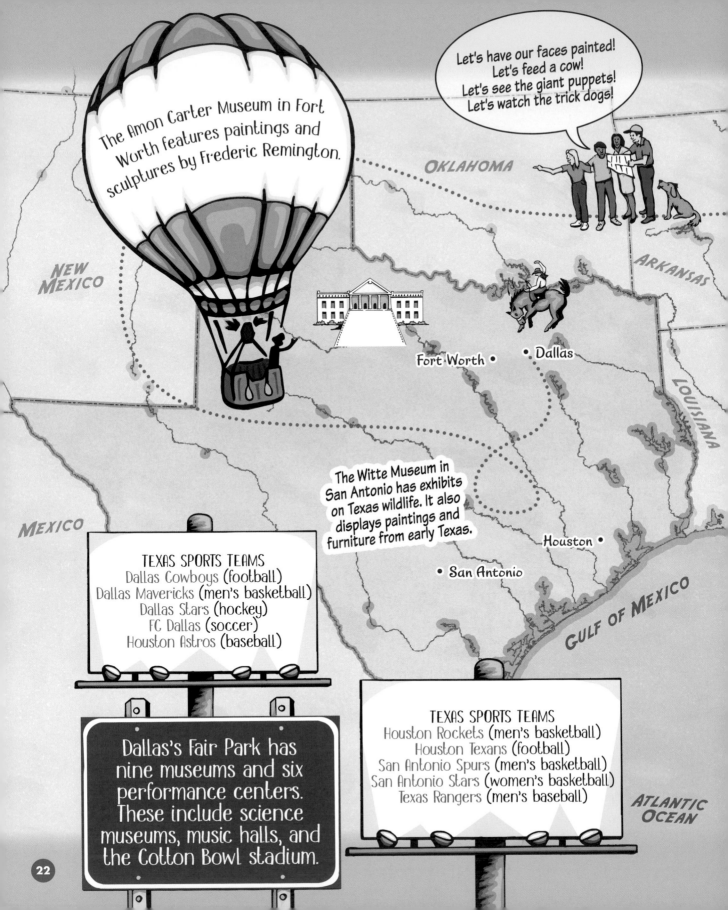

The Amon Carter Museum in Fort Worth features paintings and sculptures by Frederic Remington.

Let's have our faces painted!
Let's feed a cow!
Let's see the giant puppets!
Let's watch the trick dogs!

OKLAHOMA

NEW MEXICO

ARKANSAS

Fort Worth •   • Dallas

LOUISIANA

The Witte Museum in San Antonio has exhibits on Texas wildlife. It also displays paintings and furniture from early Texas.

Houston •

MEXICO

TEXAS SPORTS TEAMS
Dallas Cowboys (football)
Dallas Mavericks (men's basketball)
Dallas Stars (hockey)
FC Dallas (soccer)
Houston Astros (baseball)

• San Antonio

GULF OF MEXICO

Dallas's Fair Park has nine museums and six performance centers. These include science museums, music halls, and the Cotton Bowl stadium.

TEXAS SPORTS TEAMS
Houston Rockets (men's basketball)
Houston Texans (football)
San Antonio Spurs (men's basketball)
San Antonio Stars (women's basketball)
Texas Rangers (men's baseball)

ATLANTIC OCEAN

THE TEXAS STATE FAIR IN DALLAS

Animal shows, cattle barns, concerts, and yummy food. Where can you find these all in one place? At the Texas State Fair! It's held every fall in Dallas's Fair Park.

The state fair is Texas's biggest event. About two million people attend every year. And it lasts more than three weeks!

Rodeos are popular events in Texas, too. People come to show off their cowboy skills. They ride bucking horses and rope cattle.

Cowboys are an important part of life in Texas. Many Texans dress like cowboys and cowgirls. They wear boots, cowboy hats, and big belt buckles!

Watch calf roping at the Texas State Fair.

THE POTEET STRAWBERRY FESTIVAL

Strawberries dipped in chocolate. Strawberries swimming in whipped cream. Strawberries piled high on cakes. Does this sound like your kind of fun? Then head for the Poteet Strawberry Festival!

This festival celebrates a delicious Texas crop. But cotton is the top crop. No other state grows more cotton than Texas. The Rio Grande valley has a warm climate. Farmers there grow many crops. They can even grow crops in the winter.

Texas has more farmland than any other state. Much of that land belongs to cattle ranches. Beef cattle graze across vast stretches of grassland. Texas cowboys are as busy as ever today. They rope, brand, and round up cattle.

Strawberries take a couple of months to grow before they are ripe.

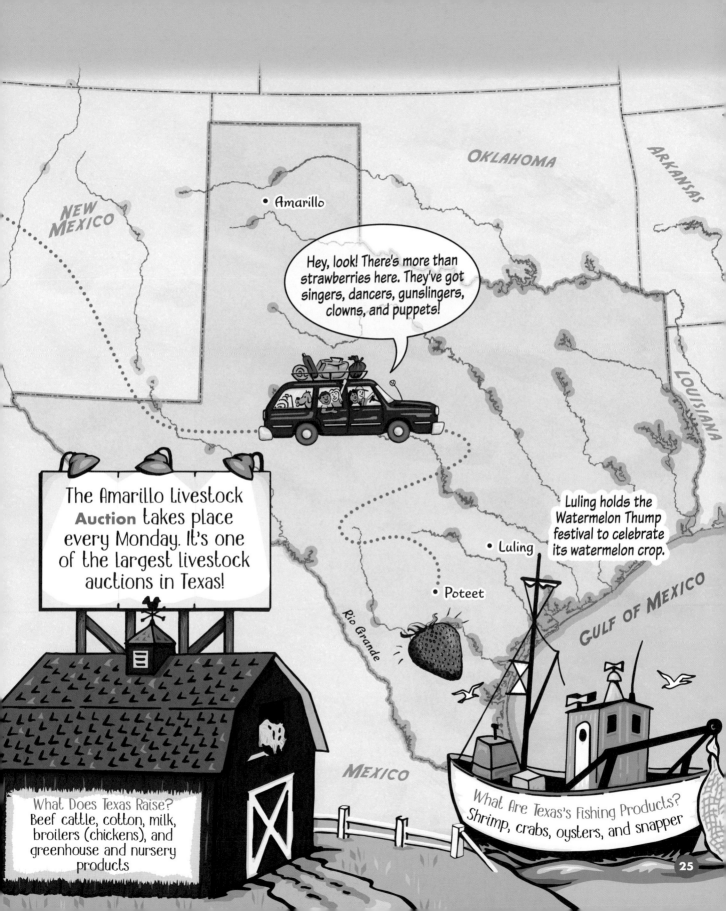

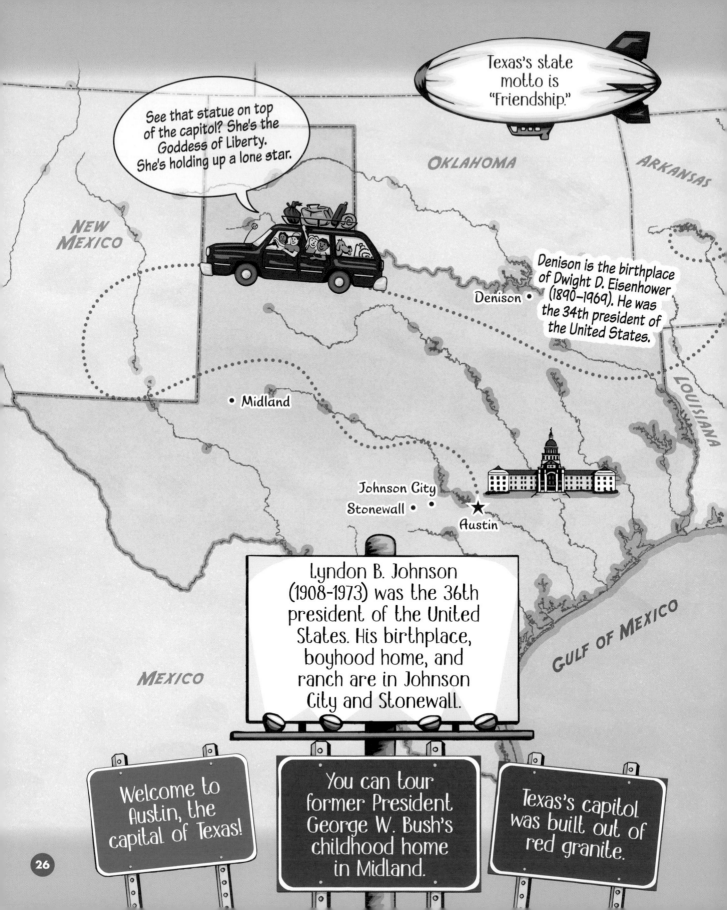

Texans like to say everything's bigger in Texas. When you see the capitol in Austin, you'll agree. It's the biggest state capitol in the country. It's taller than the U.S. Capitol in Washington, DC.

Many state government offices are in the capitol. There are three branches of government. One makes the laws. Another branch carries out the laws. It's headed by the governor. The third branch is made up of judges. They study the law. Then they apply it in courts. They decide if someone has broken the law.

Texas's capitol building took almost seven years to build.

Walk the streets of an oil **boom town**. Pump your own gas at the gas station. Ride an elevator deep into the Earth. There you'll see where oil deposits lie.

You're exploring the East Texas Oil Museum in Kilgore! It brings the oil boom days to life.

The Spindletop oil well opened in 1901. It was near Beaumont, on the Gulf Coast. Suddenly, oil became a booming **industry**. Many **oil fields** contained natural gas, too.

People kept finding more oil around the state. The biggest discovery was the East Texas oil field. It was found near Kilgore in 1930.

Texas's oil fields produced 1.1 billion barrels of oil in 2016.

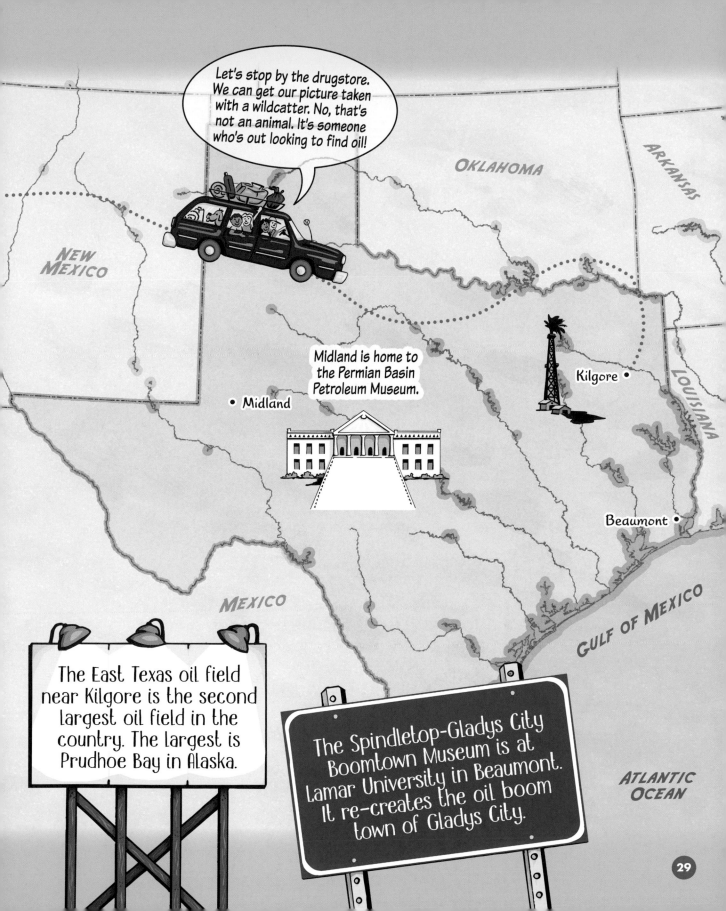

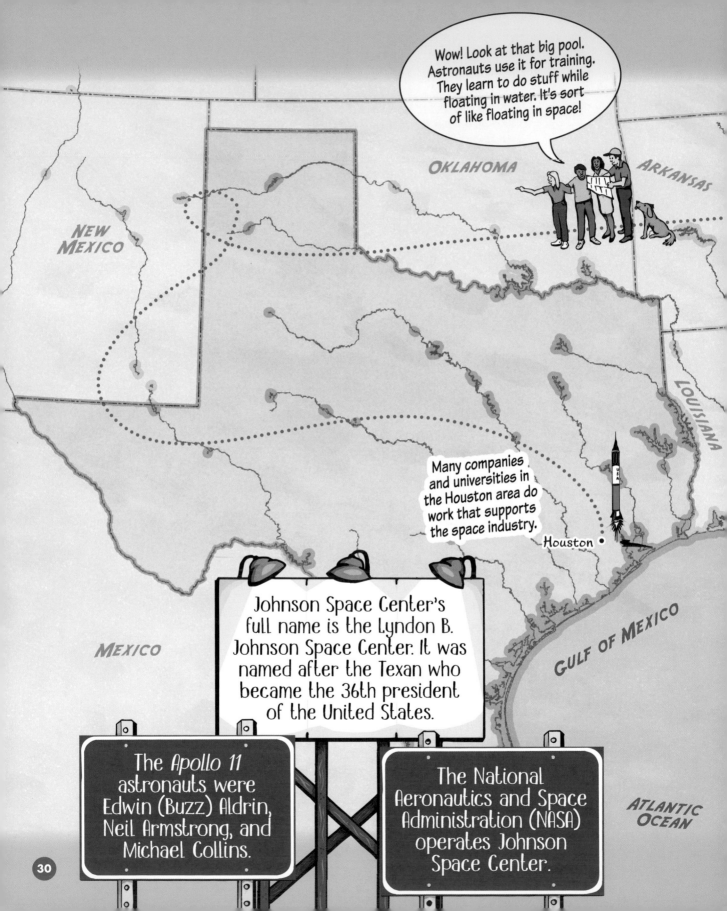

Hop on a Moon **rover**. See what a space voyage is like. You're visiting Space Center Houston! It's part of Johnson Space Center. That's where astronauts are trained.

Texas grew fast in the 1900s. Oil was just one of its booming industries. Another big business was the space industry.

Johnson Space Center began as the Manned Spacecraft Center. It was established in 1961. It directed space flights that had humans aboard. The center took a big step in 1969. It sent *Apollo 11* into space. Its astronauts were the first people on the Moon!

Johnson Space Center is one of NASA's largest research facilities.

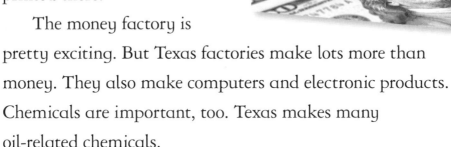

THE BUREAU OF ENGRAVING AND PRINTING IN FORT WORTH

Want to tour a money factory? Just visit the Bureau of Engraving and Printing. Its Western Currency Facility is in Fort Worth. It prints paper money for the U.S. government. You'll see billions of dollars being printed there!

The money factory is pretty exciting. But Texas factories make lots more than money. They also make computers and electronic products. Chemicals are important, too. Texas makes many oil-related chemicals.

Speaking of oil, let's not forget mining. Texas is the number-one mining state. That's because Texas mines so much oil and gas.

The Bureau of Engraving and Printing designs and makes paper money.

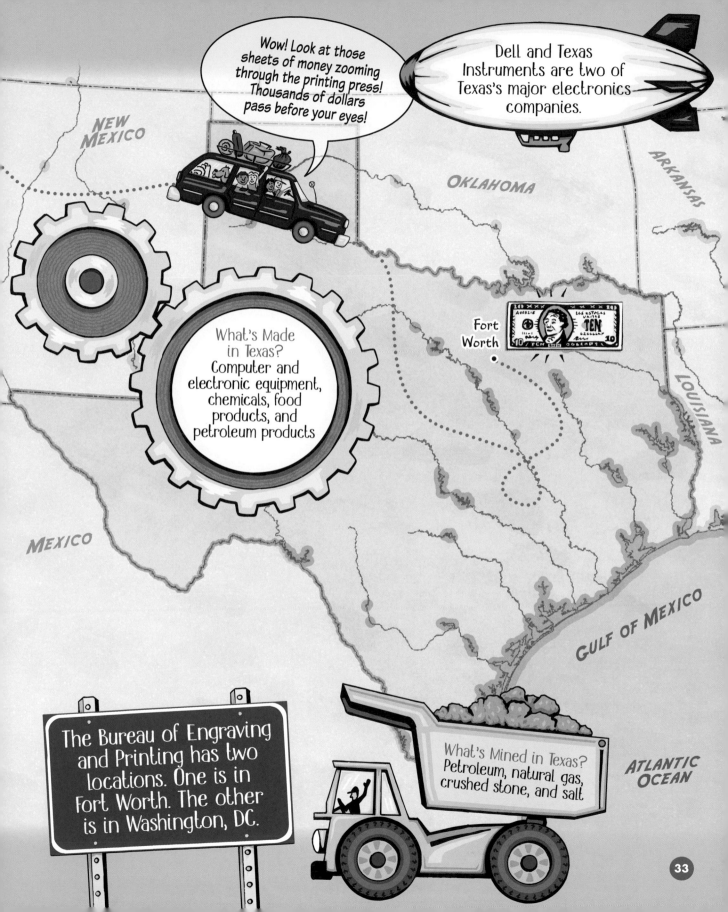

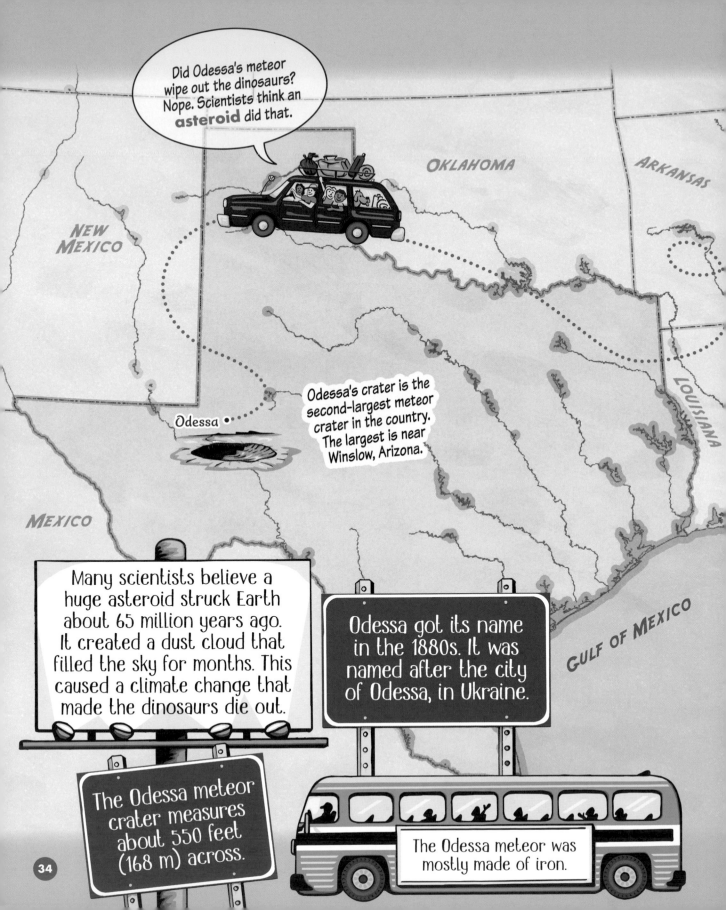

Did Odessa's meteor wipe out the dinosaurs? Nope. Scientists think an **asteroid** did that.

OKLAHOMA

ARKANSAS

NEW MEXICO

Odessa's crater is the second-largest meteor crater in the country. The largest is near Winslow, Arizona.

Odessa •

LOUISIANA

MEXICO

Many scientists believe a huge asteroid struck Earth about 65 million years ago. It created a dust cloud that filled the sky for months. This caused a climate change that made the dinosaurs die out.

Odessa got its name in the 1880s. It was named after the city of Odessa, in Ukraine.

GULF OF MEXICO

The Odessa meteor crater measures about 550 feet (168 m) across.

The Odessa meteor was mostly made of iron.

ODESSA'S METEOR CRATER

Pow! The **meteor** crashes with a deafening thud. Earth trembles and shakes. Dust clouds swirl up and fill the sky.

Luckily, you're not watching this. You might not have survived! It happened about 25,000 years ago. Now all that's left is the meteor's crater. It's a big, bowl-shaped hole near Odessa.

You won't see the meteor itself. It broke apart when it landed. Hundreds of meteor pieces have been found nearby.

Check out the Meteor Crater Museum at the crater site. You'll learn all about the Odessa meteor. You'll also learn about other materials from space.

Stop by the Meteor Crater Museum to learn more about the crater.

OUR TRIP

We visited many amazing places on our trip! We also met a lot of interesting people along the way. Look at the map below. Use your finger to trace all the places we have been.

Where is the Texas Panhandle? *See page 6 for the answer.*

Where is the Texas State Aquarium located? *Page 9 has the answer.*

Who led the first legal U.S. settlers into Texas? *See page 14 for the answer.*

What is a charro? *Look on page 18 for the answer.*

What side did Texas join during the Civil War? *Page 21 has the answer.*

What is one of Texas's largest cattle auctions? *Look on page 25 to find out!*

Who were the *Apollo 11* astronauts? *Turn to page 30 for the answer.*

STATE SYMBOLS

State bird: Mockingbird

State dish: Chili

State fiber and fabric: Cotton

State fish: Guadalupe bass

State flower: Bluebonnet

State flying mammal: Mexican free-tailed bat

State folk dance: Square dance

State fruit: Texas red grapefruit

State gem: Texas blue topaz

State insect: Monarch butterfly

State large mammal: Longhorn

State pepper: Jalapeño

State plant: Prickly pear cactus

State reptile: Horned lizard

State shell: Lightning whelk

State shrub: Crape myrtle

State small mammal: Armadillo

State sport: Rodeo

State tree: Pecan

State vegetable: Sweet onion

STATE SONG

"TEXAS, OUR TEXAS"

*Words by William J. Marsh and Gladys Yoakum Wright;
music by William J. Marsh*

Texas, our Texas! All hail the
mighty State!
Texas, our Texas! So wonderful
so great!
Boldest and grandest,
Withstanding ev'ry test;
O Empire wide and glorious,
You stand supremely blest.

Chorus:
God bless you Texas! And keep
you brave and strong,
That you may grow in power and
worth, Thro'out the ages long.

Texas, O Texas! Your freeborn
single star,
Sends out its radiance to nations
near and far.
Emblem of freedom! It sets our
hearts aglow,
With thoughts of San Jacinto and
glorious Alamo.

(Chorus)

Texas, dear Texas! From tyrant
grip now free,
Shines forth in splendor your star
of destiny!
Mother of heroes! We come your
children true,
Proclaiming our allegiance, our
faith, our love for you.

(Chorus)

State flag

State seal

That was a great trip! We have traveled all over Texas! There are a few places that we didn't have time for, though. Next time, we plan to visit the Congress Avenue Bridge in Austin. It's also known as the Bat Bridge. Visitors gather there from March through November. Every night, they watch 1.5 million Mexican free-tailed bats come out to hunt mosquitoes.

FAMOUS PEOPLE

Austin, Stephen F. (1793–1836), American pioneer who brought U.S. settlers to Texas

Bishop, Eric Morton "Jamie Foxx" (1967–), actor, singer, and comedian

Bond, Felicia (1952–), children's book author and illustrator

Burnett, Carol (1933–), actor and comedian

Bush, George W. (1946–), 43rd U.S. president

Clarkson, Kelly (1982–), singer, actress, and author

Cronkite, Walter (1916–2009), journalist and television newscaster

Gates, Melinda (1949–), philanthropist

Gomez, Selena (1992–), actress and singer

Houston, Samuel (1793–1863), soldier and politician

Johnson, Lyndon B. (1908–1973), 36th U.S. president

Johnson, Michael (1967–), track star and Olympic gold medalist

Jonas, Nick (1992–), singer, producer, and actor

Knowles, Beyoncé (1981–), singer and songwriter

Marshall, James (1942–1992), children's author and illustrator

McConaughey, Matthew (1969–), actor

Parker, Quanah (ca. 1845–1911), leader of the Comanche Native Americans

Peterson, Adrian (1985–), professional football player

Petty, Richard (1937–), NASCAR driver

Roddenberry, Gene (1921–1991), creator of *Star Trek*

Ryan, Nolan (1947–), baseball Hall of Fame pitcher

WORDS TO KNOW

asteroid (AS-ter-oid) a small rocky body orbiting the sun

auction (AWK-shuhn) a sale where people bid or offer money for something

boom town (BOOM TOUN) a town that grew up quickly because of a new business

culture (KUHL-chur) a group of people's special customs, beliefs, and way of life

enchiladas (en-chuh-LA-duhz) tortillas wrapped around a filling and covered with sauce

industry (IN-duh-stree) a type of business

legal (LEE-guhl) allowed by the law

legend (LEJ-uhnd) a story told from long ago

meteor (MEE-tee-ur) pieces of rock or other material from space that come close to Earth

missions (MISH-uhnz) centers set up for spreading a faith

oil fields (OIL FEELDZ) regions where oil lies underground

pueblo (PWEB-loh) a Native American village

reservation (rez-ur-VAY-shuhn) land set aside for a special use, such as for Native Americans

rover (ROH-vur) a vehicle that travels across land to gather information

traditions (truh-DISH-uhnz) customs passed down over many years

TO LEARN MORE

IN THE LIBRARY

Dennis, Yvonne Wakim. *A Kid's Guide to Native American History*. Chicago, IL: Chicago Review Press, 2010.

Gibson, Karen Bush. *Texas History for Kids: Lone Star Lives and Legends, with 21 Activities*. Chicago, IL: Chicago Review Press, 2015.

Gimpel, Diane Marczely. *Lyndon B. Johnson*. Mankato, MN: Child's World, 2017.

ON THE WEB

Visit our Web site for links about Texas:

childsworld.com/links

Note to Parents, Teachers, and Librarians: We routinely verify our Web links to make sure they are safe and active sites. So encourage your readers to check them out!

PLACES TO VISIT OR CONTACT

The Bullock Texas State History Museum

thestoryoftexas.com
1800 Congress Avenue
Austin, TX 78701
512/936-8746

For more information about the history of Texas

Texas Tourism

traveltexas.com
1100 San Jacinto
Austin, TX 78701
512/463-2000

For more information about traveling in Texas

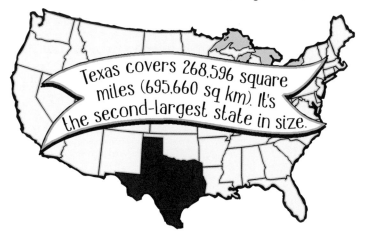

Texas covers 268,596 square miles (695,660 sq km). It's the second-largest state in size.

INDEX

A

Alamo, 16, 17
Aldrin, Edwin "Buzz," 30
Amarillo Livestock Auction, 25
Apollo 11 (spacecraft), 30, 31
Aransas National Wildlife Refuge, 9
Armstrong, Neil, 30
Austin, 26, 27

B

Battle of San Jacinto, 16, 17
Beaumont, 28, 29
Big Bend National Park, 8
boom towns, 28, 29
Brownsville, 6, 19
Bureau of Engraving and Printing, 32, 33
burrowing owls, 11
Bush, George W., 26

C

Caddoan Mounds, 13
cattle auctions, 25
cattle drives, 21
Charro Days, 19
charro, 19
Civil War, 21
Collins, Michael, 30
Confederate States of America, 21
Corpus Christi, 9
cotton, 24
Cotton Bowl stadium, 22
cowboys, 20, 23, 24
cowgirls, 23
craters, 34, 35

D

Del Rio, 6

E

East Texas oil field, 28
East Texas Oil Museum, 28, 29
El Paso, 6, 12
elevation, 6
Elkins Ranch, 20, 21

F

Fair Park, 22, 23
FC Dallas soccer team, 22
Fiesta San Antonio, 18
fiestas, 18, 19
foods, 19, 23
Fort Worth, 32, 33

G

Gladys City, 29
governors, 27
Guadalupe Peak, 6

H

Hispanics, 19
Houston, 18, 22, 30, 31
Houston, Sam, 16
Huizar, Pedro, 14

J

javelinas, 8
Johnson City, 26
Johnson, Lyndon B., 26, 30
Johnson Space Center, 30, 31
judges, 27

K

Kilgore, 28, 29

L

Laredo, 6, 18
Livingston, 13
Lubbock, 10, 11

M

Manned Spacecraft Center, 31
Matamoras, Mexico, 19
Meteor Crater Museum, 35
meteors, 34, 35
Midland, 26
mining, 32, 33
Mission San Antonio de Valero, 17
Mission San José, 14, 15
missions, 12, 14, 15, 17

N

National Aeronautics and Space Administration (NASA), 30
national parks, 6, 8, 9
Native Americans, 12, 13, 15
natural gas, 28, 32, 33
natural resources, 32, 33

O

Odessa, 34, 35
oil industry, 28, 29, 31, 32

P

Padre Island, 7
Padre Island National Seashore, 7
Panhandle, 6
population, 18
Poteet Strawberry Festival, 24
prairie dogs, 10, 11

Q

Queen of the Missions, 15

R

ranches, 20, 24, 26
Republic of Texas, 16
Rio Grande, 7, 8, 24
Rockport, 9
rodeos, 23
Rose Window, 14

S

San Antonio, 15, 16, 18, 22
San Jacinto Monument, 17
Space Center Houston, 31
space industry, 30, 31
Spanish exploration, 12
Spanish Mexico, 14, 15
Spindletop oil well, 28
Spindletop-Gladys City Boomtown Museum, 29
sports teams, 22
state bird, 9
state capitol, 26, 27
state flower, 9
state government, 27
state nickname, 17
state tree, 9
statehood, 21

T

Tex-Mex food, 19
Texas Ranger Hall of Fame and Museum, 21
Texas Rangers, 20, 21
Texas State Fair, 23

W

Washington's Birthday celebration, 18
Western Currency Facility, 32

Y

Ysleta del Sur Pueblo, 12

Bye, Lone Star State. We had a great time. We'll come back soon!